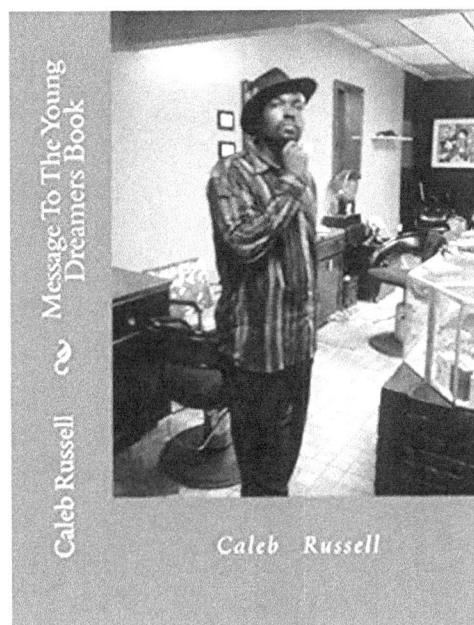

See all 2 images

The Russell Hustle Business Book

By

Caleb Russell

You must have self-discipline to be a successful Entrepreneur.

You have to save for the future.

You must be wise to make a professional,powerful,and organized budget.

You must be strong , and intelligent to write a business plan ,and stay committed to it.

It will be days you feel like stopping, but you must press on, and pray.

Establishing a company is not easy,it requires a lot of research.

You must obtain a business name so you can establish your own unique company.

Be smart ,and know the the tax laws of your state.

Choose a legal business structure that best serves you.

You must be a leader with lots of inspiration.

Don't give up rise up above all your problems,and go after your dreams .

Fund yourself raise capital independently.

Invest in your dreams, with your time, money, and mind.

Be organized, and stay focused on your your financial goals.

Think like a billionaire in order to be one.

Do lots of research on financial accounting.

Influence your friends , and family and new people you meet to build a business organization.

Save every dollar down to the penny.

Speak life , and victory to yourself ,and your business.

Visualize ,and rise,hope ,and cope.

Believe you can make it as a business owner.

Surround yourself with ambitious ,and intelligent individuals.who can contribute to your business.

Think like a business owner, and act like an entrepreneur

,save like a millionaire. Make sure you study economics, and financial accounting.

Trust , and serve God ,and you will have strength to make it as an entrepreneur.

Be your own competition.

You must focus on self-improvement everyday.

Treat your clients, employees, and business partners like royalty.

28

29

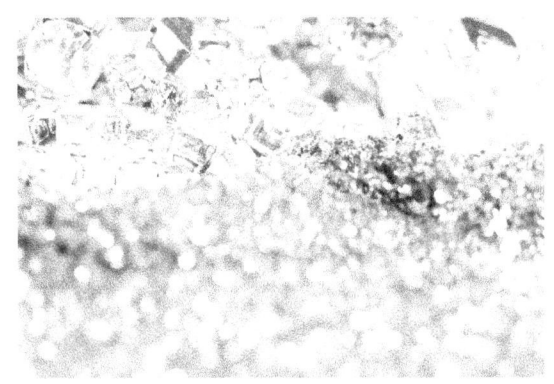

30

31
God is our provider

There is no reason to beg or borrow from other people
Or have sorrow.

God is able to provide for us today ,and tomorrow and

Forever so never give up on your dreams of success.

God is our father, therefore we are forever blessed ,and

rich.

www.ingramcontent.com/pod-product-compliance
Lightning Source LLC
Chambersburg PA
CBHW070522220526
45467CB00002B/808